Real-Life Royalty

By Starshine Roshell

The
Child's
World®
www.childsworld.com

Published in the United States of America by The Child's World®
1980 Lookout Drive • Mankato, MN 56003-1705
800-599-READ • www.childsworld.com

ACKNOWLEDGMENTS

The Child's World®: Mary Berendes, Publishing Director

Produced by Shoreline Publishing Group LLC
President / Editorial Director: James Buckley, Jr.
Designer: Tom Carling, carlingdesign.com
Cover Design: Slimfilms

Photo Credits
Cover–Rex USA (main); Corbis (Queen Elizabeth); Getty Images
(other insets).
Interior–AP/Wide World: 21; Corbis: 10, 11, 12, 13, 14, 17, 18, 19, 22,
25, 26, 27; dreamstime.com: 6, 7, 9; Getty Images: 23, 24; iStock: 15;
Photos.com: 5.

LIBRARY OF CONGRESS CATALOG-IN-PUBLICATION DATA

Roshell, Starshine.
  Real-life royalty / by Starshine Roshell.
     p. cm. — (Reading rocks!)
  Includes index.
  ISBN-13: 978-1-59296-869-5 (lib. bound : alk. paper)
  ISBN-10: 1-59296-869-4 (lib. bound : alk. paper)
  1. Kings and rulers—Biography—Juvenile literature. 2. Courts
and courtiers—Juvenile literature. I. Title. II. Series.

D106.R67 2007
929.7—dc22

                                    2007004195

CONTENTS

KINGS AND Queens

People have been interested in royal families for many years. Even if your country isn't ruled by royals, you probably still wonder about the lives of the folks with the crowns.

Since ancient times, kings and queens have ruled countries across the globe. Some royal rulers became famous for their great courage or fairness. Others are barely remembered at all. Some wore crowns and jewels to show their power. Others wore beads or feathers.

Long-ago kings and queens were often the subjects of paintings, sculptures, and other artwork.

Most have led **glamorous** lifestyles—sitting on thrones, visiting far-off lands, and dancing in ballrooms.

How do you become a king or a queen? Pure luck. The best way is if your parents are royal. Then you would be a prince or a princess. Someday, when the head of the family leaves the throne, you would become king or queen.

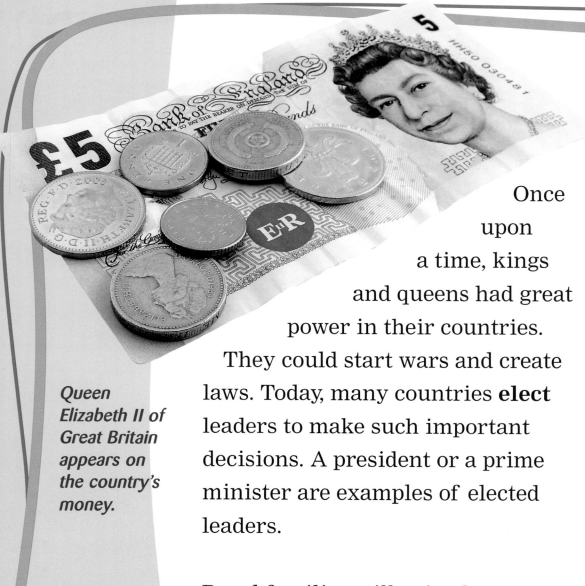

Queen Elizabeth II of Great Britain appears on the country's money.

Once upon a time, kings and queens had great power in their countries. They could start wars and create laws. Today, many countries **elect** leaders to make such important decisions. A president or a prime minister are examples of elected leaders.

Royal families still exist, however. Many still live in beautiful palaces, but few of them actually rule their land. Instead, they spend their days greeting other countries' leaders, taking part in national celebrations, visiting schools and hospitals, and attending other events.

Pictures of kings and queens appear on coins and paper money all over the world. Their faces—and the stories about their exciting lives—remind people of each country's long and interesting history.

Egypt's Pharaohs

Two of ancient Egypt's most famous rulers were very young when they **inherited** the throne. Cleopatra was only 17 when she became the queen of Egypt more than 2,000 years ago. Tutankhamen, known as King Tut, was was just nine years old!

Nothing says "royalty" like a big, glorious castle! But kings and queens aren't the only ones who live there. Palaces are home to lots of servants, and often include fancy offices and rooms for meeting with visitors.

Some of today's wealthiest people are King Abdullah of Saudi Arabia, King Bhumibol Adulyadej of Thailand, Queen Elizabeth II of England, and Queen Beatrix of the Netherlands.

The Sultan of Brunei is the king of a small country in Southeast Asia. He has the largest palace in the world. It has shiny golden domes on top, 18 elevators, and a garage that holds 110 cars!

Buckingham Palace features an enormous garden with a lake and 30 different types of birds.

Many royals enjoy lives of terrific **luxury**. Queen Elizabeth II spends most of her time at Buckingham Palace in London. This 775-room building has been home to England's royalty for 170 years. It houses many treasures, including the world's biggest pink diamond and drawings by famous artist Leonardo da Vinci.

Fancy food, beautiful clothing, lots of jewels, big, long cars... all these expensive things and more add up to luxury.

Long ago, people believed that kings and queens were like gods. **Commoners** looked up to them and wished they could be like them. Even today, the public loves to see what royals are wearing and who they are dating.

Because so many eyes are watching them, most royal families have strict rules about how to behave in public. But not all royals follow these rules.

The 18th-century French queen Marie Antoinette was a bit of a spoiled brat. French **monarch** Louis XIV liked to greet his royal visitors while he was in the bathroom. On the day King George IV of England was crowned, he wouldn't even let his wife, Caroline, into the church. She stood outside, banging on the door in her **tiara**!

Monaco's Princess Stephanie was pretty wild during her teenage years.

Modern-day royalty sometimes has troubles, too. Monaco's Princess Stephanie is known for her wild streak. Most royals are discouraged from getting tattoos— but Stephanie has three!

While some royal rulers got in trouble, others have won great respect by breaking with tradition and doing things their own way.

King Chulalongkorn was one of Thailand's most popular rulers. He

The Japanese used to believe their leaders were gods. Today, Emperor Akihito is still beloved as a symbol of his nation.

was known as "The Great Beloved King." Around 1900, he modernized his nation. He ended slavery and built railroads.

Japan's current Emperor Akihito surprised his family by marrying a commoner. Then he and Empress Michiko raised their three children themselves. (They did so instead of allowing servants to do it, as Japanese rulers before them had done.)

Rania became queen of Jordan in 1999. Her husband became king following the death of his father.

And though men make most of the decisions in her country, young Queen Rania of Jordan works hard for women's rights.

Kings and queens have been around for so long, experts say everyone on Earth is related to someone in a royal family. For example, actress Brooke Shields is a descendant of King Edward III, who ruled England during the 14th century.

It's a tradition for kings and queens to give their children names that have been in the family for centuries. Even modern royals, like Queen Margarethe II of Denmark or King Muhammad VI of Morocco, share names with their **ancestors**.

Growing up in palaces, royal children are surrounded by great riches from an early age. They wear the finest clothes, attend the best schools, and have servants to cook for them and clean their rooms.

And there isn't a toy made that their families can't afford! Now let's meet some of these kids who were born into the most royal of families.

No rowboats for royals! Royal families enjoy some of the world's biggest and fanciest yachts.

2

POWERFUL Princes

When you're a prince, growing up doesn't have to mean giving up your toys. Lots of princes have collections of sports cars, racehorses, or ships.

Being the **heir** to a throne is a lot of work, but princes know how to have fun, too. Prince Azim of Brunei flew pop star Monica to his Asian island just to sing at his birthday party.

Lots of princes play sports. Prince Albert of Monaco has a black belt in judo karate, and he competed five times in Olympic bobsledding. Prince Harry of England loves polo and rugby. Twin princes Philip and Alexander of Yugoslavia like to scuba dive.

England's Prince Harry (left) and Prince William take a breather after a polo match. Polo is a game played on horseback.

Being a prince means more than just having fun. Besides studying history, math, and other subjects, princes must learn to be strong leaders. They also have to understand their country's **politics** so they can help run it some day.

The military teaches princes both skills. England's Prince Charles trained as a fighter pilot in the Royal Air Force and is an admiral of the Royal Navy. His sons, William and Harry, are officers of the English army.

A prince in ski clothing: the popular and handsome Prince Felipe hits the slopes.

Some princes go to college in other countries to learn about the rest of the world. It's easier to study in a place where you're not so famous. Prince Felipe of Spain and his cousin, Prince Pavlos of Greece, were roommates while they went to Georgetown University in the United States.

3

REAL-LIFE
Princesses

What little girl doesn't dream of being a princess? Even if she's not born into a royal family, a girl can become a princess by marrying a prince. That dream came true for American movie star Grace Kelly. She fell in love with Prince Rainier III of Monaco when she was 26 years old. In 1956, they had a fairy-tale wedding, and she stopped making movies.

The couple lived with their three children in a pink palace with more than 200 rooms.

Located on top of a hill, it gave the family beautiful views of the Mediterranean Sea. Princess Grace loved her royal life, but she still enjoyed doing everyday things, too. She cooked many of her family's meals—especially breakfast—and visited the United States often.

The world watched in wonder as the beautiful actress Grace Kelly married the dashing Prince of Monaco.

The wedding of Prince Charles and Princess Diana in 1981 was like something out of a storybook.

One of the world's most famous princesses was Diana, Princess of Wales. As a girl, Diana was a singer and athlete who hoped to one day become a ballerina. She was teaching kindergarten when she met England's Prince Charles, who asked her to marry him. A billion people watched their wedding in 1981. Shy, 20-year-old Diana wore a shimmering silk dress and a diamond tiara.

Often called "The People's Princess," Diana spent a lot of time helping people who were sick or hurt. She worked with more than 100 **charities**, including many that helped children. She and Charles divorced in 1992, which meant she could no longer be called "princess." Diana died in 1997.

Diana used her fame to help children in need around the world.

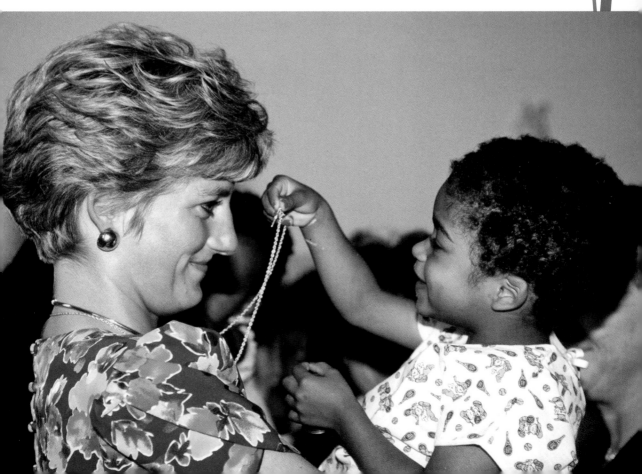

In storybooks, princesses are often rescued from monsters or fire-breathing dragons. But today's royal women are not helpless girls. In fact, they work hard to help people less **fortunate** than themselves. Their fame helps bring attention to problems. Being famous gives them the chance to do good.

Queen Rania and Princess Inaara joined forces at this charity event in 2004.

Princess Elizabeth of Yugoslavia created a charity that brings medicine and clothing to people whose countries are at war. Princess Haya of Jordan helps bring food to hungry nations all over the world.

Sweden's Princess Madeleine uses her role to help the less fortunate.

Princess Madeleine of Sweden raises money to grant wishes to children with cancer, and Princess Inaara works to bring money to poor parts of the world. She also works to help people with diseases such as AIDS, and to find loving homes for abused dogs. Princess Kiko of Japan represents the work of the Red Cross in her country.

Princess Letizia learned good speaking skills as a reporter and uses them as a princess.

Some people think that a warm smile and a graceful wave is all a princess needs to do in public. But princesses like to use their brains, too!

Princess Letizia of Spain was a television news reporter before she married Prince Felipe. Princess Märtha Louise of Norway has

Boys vs. Girls

For centuries, many royal families had rules that only sons—not daughters—could take over the throne. But that is beginning to change. Sweden, Norway, and Belgium all have new rules that allow a ruler's oldest child to wear the crown—whether that person is a prince or a princess.

This 1962 photo shows Princess Elizabeth with her father, George Rukidi. He was the Omukama (King) of the Toro Kingdom of Uganda.

written a children's book about her family's history. Princess Kiko of Japan knows sign language and uses her skills to help hearing-challenged people and hearing people understand each other. Princess Elizabeth of Toro was Uganda's first female lawyer, and later became a fashion model!

Fashion and princesses fit together like a glass slipper onto Cinderella's foot. Never mind velvet robes and pointy princess hats—modern royals like to step out in style!

Famous fashion designers sometimes send dresses to princesses for special parties. And some princesses even design their own dresses!

Burundi is a nation in Central Africa. Though it has a president now, it used to have a royal family. Esther Katamari is a princess of that family.

Princess Marie-Chantal of Greece and Thailand's Princess Siriwanwaree design clothing for themselves and others. Princess Angela of Liechtenstein worked for a fashion designer at one time.

Royal Blue?

In ancient times, the color purple became a symbol of royalty. That's because purple clothing dye was so expensive that only kings and queens could afford it. In some African countries, yellow is considered royal because it is the color of gold.

Esther Katamari, princess of Burundi, worked as a fashion model for many years.

Esther posed in this beautiful gown . . . like a princess!

Kings and queens, princes and princesses . . . they come out of the pages of history to live in our world today. But today's world is much more than tall castle towers and beautiful coaches. Here's hoping your royal dreams come true someday, too.

GLOSSARY

ancestors   people who came before you in your family

charities   organizations that collect money and use that money to help people in different ways

commoners   everyday, non-royal people

elect   to choose someone for a job by voting for him or her

fortunate   having good luck

glamorous   beautiful and luxurious

heir   a person who receives someone's title, money, or property when that person dies

inherited   received someone's title, money, or property when that person died

luxury   expensive things that are enjoyable, but not needed

monarch   a single ruler, such as a king, queen, or emperor

politics   the way a government is run

tiara   a small crown worn by female royals

FIND OUT MORE

BOOKS

Kristina: The Girl King, Sweden 1638 (Royal Diaries)
by Catherine Meyer (Scholastic, 2003).
A popular fiction series based on the life of a real Swedish
royal family.

Princess Diana
by Joanne Mattern (DK, 2006).
An in-depth, illustrated biography of the late Princess of
Wales.

A Princess Primer
by Stephanie True Peters (Dutton Juvenile, 2006).
Written by a "fairy godmother," this book focuses more on the
fairy-tale princesses.

To Be a Princess
by Hugh Brewster (Harper Collins, 2001).
The stories of 12 real-life princesses, from ancient to modern
times, including details of what their lives were like in their
castles and palaces.

WEB SITES

Visit our Web page for lots of links about real-life royalty:
www.childsworld.com/links

Note to Parents, Teachers, and Librarians: We routinely check our Web links to
make sure they're safe, active sites—so encourage your readers to check them out!

INDEX

STARSHINE ROSHELL writes a funny newspaper column about her life for the Santa Barbara (Calif.) *Independent*. She contributes to national magazines and Web sites and helps keep track of her active kids, Stone and Dash.